My Coney Island

poems by

Susan E. Oringel

Finishing Line Press
Georgetown, Kentucky

My Coney Island

Copyright © 2019 by Susan E. Oringel
ISBN 978-1-63534-946-7 First Edition
All rights reserved under International and Pan-American Copyright Conventions. No part of this book may be reproduced in any manner whatsoever without written permission from the publisher, except in the case of brief quotations embodied in critical articles and reviews.

ACKNOWLEDGMENTS

"Olive Juice," "Romance Alfómbrico" and "My Miłosz Dream" were published in the NCTE *English Journal*
"The Message" was published in *Crania: A Journal of Literature and Art*
 "Not Just Any Old Food" won second prize in the Michael Egan Poetry Contest and was published in the Summer 1994 issue of the *Maryland Poetry Review*

Publisher: Leah Maines
Editor: Christen Kincaid
Cover Art: Wonder Wheel, Coney Island: Found Images Press Inc., foundimage.com; Family Photo: Susan E. Oringel
Author Photo: Deborah Foss
Cover Design: Jackie Steelman and Marta Jaremko

Printed in the USA on acid-free paper.
Order online: www.finishinglinepress.com
 also available on amazon.com

Author inquiries and mail orders:
Finishing Line Press
P. O. Box 1626
Georgetown, Kentucky 40324
U. S. A.

Table of Contents

Song of Coney Island 1
Not Just Any Old Food 2
My Father's War 3
Nathan's Hot Dog Eating Contest 4
Pink Balloon 5
My Father's Workshop 6
Playing on the Beach 7
How the Body 8
House 9
The Fact of After 10
Romance Alfómbrico 11
Traveling Through the Dark, Again 12
Poor Everybody 13
My Miłosz Dream 14
Last Responder 15
Struck 16
Last Days 18
La Vie en Gris 19
The Last Lunch 20
The Message 21
Mother Love 22
Olive Juice 23
Chopped Chicken Livers 24
Mom and Dad Barbeque in Heaven 25
Carcass 26
My Coney Island 27
Notes 28
Additional Acknowledgments 29

For
Robert Sherman Oringel
and
Beverly Feinberg Oringel

I am waiting for my case to come up and
I am waiting for a rebirth of wonder
—Lawrence Ferlinghetti

Song of Coney Island

I'm going to Coney Island, where it rains peacocks
and the lampposts are rainbow swirl lollipops.
I'll take the F train to Coney, that rabbit foot,
coney foot, lucky foot, boot of Brooklyn with its toe
in the ocean. I'll be dancing in Coney Island, with the
drag and burlesque queens in the Mermaid Parade,
men in shell brassieres and long green tails,
women in sequins and feathers. I'll be riding
in Coney Island, dizzied on the Cyclone, the Parachute Jump,
my head and stomach trading places, my mouth,
screaming, and I'll be breezing in Coney Island where my
grandpa still fishes on the pier and Grandma grinds carp
for gefilte fish. Where the beach looks like matzoh meal,
where my mother stills sits on the fire escape
of their fourth floor walk-up, reading with thick glasses
from rheumatic fever. I'll be swimming in Coney Island,
in an ocean of salty green *schav*. I'll be strolling
on the boardwalk in Coney Island, maybe all the way to
Brighton Beach. Short, big breasted Russian women in furs
and hennaed hair will be my aunts, my mother, my sister and me.
I'll be peeking in Coney Island at the freak show where a dime
will buy the two-headed lady, two-sexed baby, Siamese twins,
the world's smallest man, and in the house of magic mirrors,
I'll be wide as a doorway, thin as a line, and then I'll disappear!

Not Just Any Old Food

Coney Island, 1934, they have to call down
to the basement again for my father, ten years old,
whose hands move across the delicate innards
of radios and clocks, wires, gears, glass tubes.
Upstairs in the three room flat, one bedroom for the girls,
one for his parents, the family huddles
round the tiny kitchen table. For him
they find a folding chair out of the front closet.
There's not much for supper, Grandpa's hat business is failing
and Grandma doesn't like to cook. She slices the dry
pot roast square, biggest piece for Grandpa, the provider,
serves herself a chunk, the girls get meat like translucent
wafers to keep their black hair shiny. My father stares
out the cracked kitchen window, sees beyond the brick
of the house next door to a world filled with ruby
steak, gleaming butter, chocolate cake
and coffee ice cream. Someday he will have all
that and a honey-voiced wife who will cook for him,
all he wants. He lowers his knife
and fork to gravy on bread.

My Father's War

My father's stories made us laugh:
the time, with borrowed jeep, he crashed
into the colonel's flower bed and tent.
The basic training lemonade, fermenting
in cast iron buckets in the Georgia sun,
that sickened everyone. Running
under trees from bullets that strafed the atoll—
he made it sound more sport than dodging balls.
His one big battle: a goat had slipped
between the lines, firing broke out, the Japanese
enclosed my father's company and after hours
of rounds, the one who started it was found,
riddled, stiff on the ground.

"More fun than summer camp," he'd sigh,
"Much more fun." I liked to thumb through to find
the pages of tanned, smiling Brooklyn boys that graced
his photo album, in undershirts, dog tags, arms chained
like brothers. His sepia portrait: hat, medals, uniform,
a pastel sunset, tree and lake painted in,
his face, my face, the same cheekbones and grin.
I'd turn until the empty pages, black.
But once I found more pictures in the back,
dead soldiers strewn like flowers on the sand.

Nathan's Hot Dog Eating Contest
Coney Island, Fourth of July

If the heart is a hungry stomach, always wanting
more love, more attention, more more,
then the stomach is a heart reaching to grant that wish.
It's the only way I can understand
grown men and women cramming 65 or more
3 oz. orange tubes of processed beef (skin, fat, gristle) and pasty
pillows into their maws to win a prize. They fold the dogs and buns
("HDBs") to shove them in faster. Joey Chestnut,
Sonya "Black Widow" Thomas, Takeru Kobayashi,
Pat "Big Dish" Bertolleti—they're professional eaters,
not food addicts who eat to numb the pain, but so-called athletes.
Think of tongues doing pushups and stomachs, "downward dog."

Nathan's was the Old Country for me,
blocks away from Mom's parents on Mermaid.
My favorites were the chow mein rolls, pineapple soda,
ridged french fries in cones, and the buttery smell
of kitchen grease. (Knishes and blintzes, you had to get elsewhere.)
In the raw bar, beer in frosted mugs for adults, a man once
flirted with my mother while my sister and I giggled.

They say in 1916 two men had a hot dog duel
at Nathan's on July 4, to see who was more patriotic:
one's heart being in one's stomach, so to speak.
Now the entrants belong to the International Foundation
of Competitive Eaters and it's all televised on ESPN.

And why not? Burlesque, carnival rides, barrels and
tunnels of love, mermaid parades, midways with freaks:
Coney has always stretched the limits of what humans
can do to themselves and each other for entertainment.
For a buck. Hey, bring on the show.

Pink Balloon
    Harborplace, Baltimore

Saturday night, eating steamed crabs alone
at a wooden kiosk. When I was ten, my parents,
laughing, taught me how to flip open a crab's carapace,
tear off the legs and the lungs, the "devil fingers,"
to break the chitin-white body in two
and pull out savory entrails, buttery hunks of meat.
Tonight, not having a knife, I use
my fingernails to pry open sweet chambers
that cut my flesh. The salt and paprika sting.

Tonight, across town, my father sleeps at Johns Hopkins,
hooked to tubes, missing his kidney. This week he changed
from stuporous stranger wrapped in blankets on a gurney,
unable to feel his legs as we painted his lips with ice,
to a patient shuffling down the faintly spattered hall,
with his chirping IV pole and bags of fluids,
nodding to the other men trailing their own red and yellow bags.
My mother, shouting, paced his room; he argued back
and she flounced out, leaving us, once again.

Two booths away, a dark-haired little girl is crying. I look up
to see her reach for the ceiling, jumping, grabbing over her head.
Her grandmother laughs, points to her husband, speaks in, say,
Korean. We all look up to see a pink balloon drifting in the rafters.
The girl has lost it, and the grandparents say something, perhaps,
"You should have held tighter," or better, "Don't worry,
we'll get you another." But she doesn't want another.
She wants that one, the one she had.

My Father's Workshop

Dad pounds away and swears in the small
but organized garage. Above the spattered workbench
he's nailed baby food jars of nails and screws
to a block of wood. They swivel out from pegboard,
rattle like threats. The bench, freckled with paint,
matches his brown-spotted skin. He pounds
and swears, *Dammit!* He can't make that
sonofabitch loosen or fit together right.
He has no brother, no friends, and we
can't help. It's just hammer, screwdriver,
drill, the wrench. *Dammit!*

Playing on the Beach
    Reginald Marsh, 1947, Portland Museum of Art

Another hot white day on the Coney Island beach,
a sea of people escaping Depression's end, the war,
and city heat. Here the illustrator-painter
sketches with oils three main figures faintly fleshed in—
daubing a bit of yellow, red, and black, for bathing suits
and caps— while a chorus of musclebound shades in beige
and grays flank them behind, right and left.
.
Marsh loved to document, the placard says, places
people gathered, Coney, the Village, 14th Street,
places where old morality gave way, displayed flesh and pleasure,
like the Parisian dancers and prostitutes
painted by Degas and Toulouse-Lautrec.

Off center but foreground a man presses behind a woman,
hugs her hard under her ample breasts while the woman
reaches out to a figure who looks like her younger self.
The first woman's head is tilted back toward the man, but her
downcast expression suggests sorrow at her surrender.
As if she longs for her old innocence, a body not
tethered to another, able to skip away.

But aren't we all tethered? First to our own bodies,
then to others, to life, and finally to death, as the more
vaguely painted, surrounding bodies suggest, muscled but fading
from the scene. The other beach-goers, the museum notes,
with their "muscular and frieze-like postures suggest the
bacchanalian celebrations painted in classical times."
Yes, even the ancients craved love and ecstasy,
escape from what was, is, surely waiting.

How the Body

He doesn't see the flowers
in the blue-striped jug I've brought.
This gray-skinned stranger snores
then calls my sister's name.
Flowers are for the healthy.
The nurses coo over the cunning mums and daisies
arranged with shots of niece and nephew.

Last night my father labored to breathe.
His diaphragm, a stallion kicking down the stall,
heaved. I tried to match his efforts
in my own belly and felt
a laughing gasp, a sob.

Now he drifts in a morphine sea,
his wake, a bubbling snore,
and the intercom above his head
crackles with nurses' calls:
"Are you there?" "Forty four."
Between cells, the slashed
branches struggle again

to meet: artery, muscle, vein.
How the body must shout
its fury for the organ stolen, even though
swollen with cancer, the fisted lump
plundered from its red fields. And how the body
howls its knowing in the hollow left behind.

House

They buried Viking chieftains with their thrones,
yet Dad's leather recliner still sits
in the quiet house where all-day TV news
no longer blares, where my mother's off-key
humming, as she dusts, no longer floats.
For now this house is mine and I can do
anything, my actions unremarked upon.
So this is what it's like to be an orphan:
free in a home aching with ghosts.

The Fact of After

Stomach sucker-punched, you double over,
shaking. Face flushes, hot chills run through
your veins. Head pounds, heart pounds, you're
feeling faint and you want to scream. Maybe
you do. No. No. But the line has been drawn
between before and after and you can't
erase it. You can't go back. That line
will always be there. Your head tries to
out-think it, but it can't. It never will.
Disbelief covers you like a body bag, a shroud,
but in your thrashing, there will be rips. Pieces
of light, of the picture, will emerge,
will go from blur to clear. You rub your eyes,
but it's still there. You rage, you plead,
but nothing works. The awful fact of after
becomes the clay you keep worrying,
working on and with, over and over, kneading, pounding,
until the shape becomes something.
Something you can live with.

Romance Alfómbrico

Blue, how very deeply blue.
Blue splashed with moonlight,
blue of sea, blue sea foam.
Blue bowls, blue glasses, turquoise canning jars.

I want a magic carpet of blue
for my alchemical kitchen
whose walls are pale peach,
Serengeti sand.
Oh blue of Caribbean,
twilight poured into cream.

In my bare feet I dream them,
pale feet pad on bamboo floors
orange-brown as oak, I dream
the mother who will cook us soup,
the lover who makes my name
a song, the father who can fix all things.

Blue, how I want you blue.
Carpet of jute, cotton, wool,
not the ghostly sheen of nylon, olefin,
the mat advertised "100% miscellaneous."
Twisted from tropical trees, from my lover's
wavy strands, I want you striped,
brown and beige of earth,
white of warm sands and greeny blue, oceans.

I wait at the window in my white
night gown, beckoning the man, the rug,
splashed with the moon,
but now I am not I, nor is
my house now my house
and the man's *white shirt*
has grown thirsty dark brown roses.

Blue, how very deeply blue.

Traveling Through the Dark, Again

When I had turned onto that suburban street and saw
a hump in the twilight, I slowed,
only to watch a rabbit being thrown
from a passing car's sickening hit. *Oh, bunny.*

Nature! I can sink tuna cans in earth,
fill them with beer to drown slugs.
My compost heaps hold humus dark as devil's food
and the rictus of grapefruit and squash
and bluish rotting onions. But this, *this—*

Louder than the crickets, it gasped in little clicks,
furiously shaking its limp hind legs. It whirled and whirled,
a pinwheel in a bitter wind, beating against the walls
of death, like the walls of that restroom stall
I once hid in while my mother screamed for all to hear,
the walls that pulsed and squeezed out all my air
till I thought I'd die or go crazy; and now, I could not
kill it, could not nudge it to the side of the road.

Poor Everybody

I want a prayer for the woman who finds her beloved
naked, dead on the floor and for his ex-wife
standing at the graveside, for the driver
who has one too many just-one-mores and the parents
who lose a son and hope, a prayer for the teacher
fronting another dozing class hung over
from the midnight shift, partying away the pain,
or a baby crying till five a.m. A prayer
for the man rushing to his sixteenth job interview
who slams into the woman rushing to the hospital
to kiss her mother goodbye. For the mother
who beats her girl as her own mother beat her.

I want all the lost beloveds, hopes, and happinesses
found, shining from whatever other plane
that may exist—but what of those who don't
believe in more than just this flesh, this earth?

My Miłosz Dream

> *...how difficult it is to remain just one person,*
> *for our house is open, there are no keys in the doors,*
> *and invisible guests come in and out at will* —Czesław Miłosz

She left—the former owner—but left
junk cars and lumber on the lawn,
ball gowns and dishes dispersed
and the woodstove with incense burning.

The doors swung open to all her friends—
they didn't need keys
and came to chat about the good old days.

She even left a daughter, my old self,
a surly girl who whined each time I tried
to make it my own home. And I whined back,
I bought this place, but everyone
told me gravely, I was wrong.

A country house on a hill, acreage,
intended escape, but this was a way station
for neighbors; a tiny urban ghetto nestled close,
armies of boys wheeled around on bikes,
men in fatigues with guns darted through streets:
shouts, sounds of breaking glass.

Safe, safe, I muttered, shooing neighbors out.
I rammed an old oak table against the kitchen door,
piled up wooden chairs. Then ran and shoved the sofa
behind the front, a bureau stuffed with keepsakes
behind that. By sunset I'd hammered shut
all the windows, when I heard the knock.

An elderly voice, accented, gentle,
asked me to let him in. I sat transfixed;
he found the one door I'd forgot. Entered
in a long gray coat, kissed my forehead, and said,
Yes, it's difficult, those guests—Still, it's your house.

Last Responder
> *From an AP News Story, 2006*

He searches for fingers,
toes, bits of bone that could
fit into the puzzle of a jaw or
pelvis, leg, fragments of white or cream
smudged with char among the burned remains
of concrete, sheet rock, wood, splinters of glass.

He searches for something human
in the mountains of cracked asphalt,
wadded cardboard and paper, for a hand,
that delicate, empty basket, or a
Claddagh ring, a man's ID bracelet, something
that survived the fire, the crash, and five long years.

Retired now, this is his job. He searches
for his younger brother, a sergeant, FDNY,
of whom no trace has been found,
to snuff the flickering hope—*lost, with amnesia*—
or be granted the grace that holy relics give,
touching a piece of the once beloved.

This is all he can do.
He is a last responder. Not one of the ones
who grabbed their coats, ran, and rode,
who carried hoses, hatchets, gas masks, hammers,
colleagues, gasping victims, bodies in shock,
the ones who ran into the burning towers,
carrying wallets with credit cards and pictures,
carrying their wives and babies and the kids
at their desks in school, the mothers clutching phones,
the fathers sitting vigil in front of the television,
and the brothers and sisters who had to live on,
carrying all of us left behind.

Struck

There's three feet of blizzard in Denver
and my sister can't see the house next door,
let alone trek across town

to the hospital for my mother,
transported by emergency crew
from 9-1-1, in mid-dialysis,

but thank God, the phones still work,
so I get her terse report while in
freakishly balmy Albany

I feel my own white-out of fear
and uselessness with distance.
"They think it's a *humid*," my mother later

says, "maybe a stroke." "A *what*, Ma?" I repeat.
"A spot on my, you know, brain."
The connection buzzes and she cries,

"I told your sister, no nursing home.
If I can't live the way I want,
I'm going to die."

But a year ago, before Christmas, too,
she'd fallen, cracked her pelvis,
six months after my father died,

Christmas, their anniversary,
and the nurses said she'd never
walk again. She did.

Probably a stroke. A small one.
But five hours later, my sister
leaves a message: it's a tumor,

and a bad one: *glial blastoma*.
I see little men in hard hats
blasting sections of her brain,

uncoupling brain from speech.
And when they unhinge brain
from movement, brain, from breath, what then?

The Denver airport's closed.
I can't fly out for days.
Like Mom, I pace and wait.

Last Days

I "Sundowning"

Her pale flesh hangs in jowls with a determined
bend of head on neck and wide eyes from which
shoot a look of fear, cunning, or wonder:
"It's amazing!"
At twilight she worries whose house she's in.
Ponders why the perfumes on the dresser,
placed just the way she would,
are the ones she uses: Lovely, Youth Dew.
We tell her the trusted doctor
ordered it so. "Then who's going to pay
for all this?" And who cooked the brisket
defrosted for tonight? "You did,
Mom, when you weren't
sick." "I did?
Amazing."

II The Storms

O wonders of the world, tornadoes
in Flatbush and the gray blue bowl
of Colorado cracked with Biblical
light, day after day, as she lay
on her tossed bed, the waste
building up in her blood, the tumor
shadowing more and more of the
vessels of thought, till all
was moan, *Won't
somebody help me?* and flailing rage:
I want to kill you in your face.
But after each downpour over the parched plains,
whole rainbows would bloom like a promise
of peace: the morphine sleep and then
the final loosened breath.

La Vie en Gris

Three months after she died
I saw my mother on the movie screen
as Edith Piaf, the same wide, wild eyes,
rolling in rage, in fright, also
defiant daughter of the city's poor. I saw
the early illness, neglect that nearly blinded
each and the histories of abandonments:
Piaf's father, away at the first World War,
my grandmother a year and a half in state hospital,
and my mother had to leave high school
to tend to her dad—Piaf sang on street corners
with hers, for cash.

Raw ambition and instinct
for survival pushed them out and up, with Piaf,
from man to man, with my mother, towards
a thing I still can't name, some wanting
never quenched. Betrayals,
breakdowns, illnesses, the pills—
—the will, indomitable—my mother, 79,
sweeping the garage floor when she could
barely walk or talk, Piaf staggering
onto the stage, only to fall
again, but when she gripped the microphone
like a throat, that ringing vibrato
insisted that you listen.

The Last Lunch

"I can't say I haven't had a good life," my mother cried
on the phone, when she announced her kidney failure
and the beginning of the end. Dad, still alive then, was
a silent presence, often, on the other line. "I wanted
daughters and had two, I wanted to go to college, and finally
did, and I wanted to teach and I taught for 17 years.
Your father and I traveled all over the world. I've had
a good life." Then started to sob while my father
made soothing noises, repeating, "Beverly, stop." But a year
later he died, and another year later, she was diagnosed
with the brain tumor, and bravery turned to rage.
And the screaming that brought back my childhood.

"Half of taking care of Bev was going out to lunch with her,"
Dee, the aide, told me, as we prepared my mom—helped her dress,
got the cane—for what would be her last meal in a restaurant,
and just about her last meal. I remember almost nothing
but the place, "The Ripe Tomato," near the fancy mall,
and fixing her a plate from the salad buffet. Cherry tomatoes
and yellow squash in a vinaigrette. Pieces of veggie sushi.
Fluorescent lights. And sitting across from her with Dee
alongside me, two sisters having lunch with their mom.
She could barely talk, but was lecturing about something. Maybe
politics. I kept wanting to ask questions about her life,
about how she was feeling about her death, to feel somehow
connected. But I couldn't. For that instant, she seemed happy.

The Message

Come the first days of snow and cold,
black arms of trees, gray sky.
Inside this little house

lamb stew with roots,
baked apples, split skin bubbles juice.
I'm snug, alone.

But days go on, the north wind
howls my song, alone, alone,
abandoned now my books, the cats

growl and scratch, upturn
the rooms, there's nothing
in the fridge, I order in,

crack open sugary shells, fortunes,
toss them into night,
and shuffle off to bed, remembering

the boy who feared the dark, sleeping alone,
and was told to think of Jesus holding him.
"Yes, but I can't feel his skin."

Tonight the wish to feel skin
makes me wince. But I'll wake
to sun upon a brilliant field
on which a line of cloven prints
is carved, striding across
the glittering crystals,
wishbones, hinged like wings.

Mother Love

We never baked Christmas cookies but once:
my mother grabbed the rolling pin we'd thumped
on her pink formica counter dotted with golden stars,
her *Nice Clean Kitchen!* Flour and butter stuck
in sticky dunes, the rainbow sugars so much colored dust
swirling, her words like punctuating fists,
this time, words only. The cookies burned, of course,
the snowmen, bells, and sad, singed hearts.

But years later, the first night I babysat
for the backyard neighbors' kids, was it a warm spring night?
I opened the door—first sin—the dog sprang out
and I panicked, called my mother and she showed up
in housecoat and curlers, she, mortally afraid
of dogs or anything that walked on fours,
she rounded up that big gray barking poodle
in the dark, who knows how?
And she was shaking.

Olive Juice

I love alliteration's tricky licks and the *ahs*
of assonance—time to relax—delicious
fricatives and glottal stops. The blunt
flat hammers of *stab* and *shit!*
Those Anglo-Saxons really knew their,
er, stuff, and the polysyllabic latinates
aren't too shabby. But rhyme
that chimes, *Ay, ay, ay*, some
subtlety, puhleez! And it
amuses me how love and loathe
are close, in sound, anyway,
how "olive juice" said to someone
across a room sounds like, "I love you."
Try it. And no matter how nicely someone
says my full first name, it always
sounds like Mother scolding.

Chopped Chicken Livers

The grinder was sculpted yellow metal with a silver mouth
and black rubber feet that stuck to the counter.
Mom fried up the livers and onions in chicken fat that spat
from the frying pan and she boiled eggs in her mother's
little gray saucepan. The bloody livers would pool into muddy lumps
and the onions would be gilded with ridges of brown and black.
Grinding was my favorite part: eggs, onions, and liver
would emerge from the holes, yellow, white, and brown
worms, which Mom would mash with garlic, mayonnaise, salt.
I liked to crank the grinder and make the worms wiggle out,
worms you could eat! Disgusting. Delicious.

Mom and Dad Barbeque in Heaven

Dad, wearing the pastel-striped apron and fluffy chef's hat
we gave him for Father's Day in the sixties, wields a knife
like a knight's bright lance. Inside, Mom boils Rice-a-Roni,
smooths softened ice cream into crushed cookie crusts.
"The flavors they have here," she murmurs,
her once care-worn face, unlined, brightened.

Dad marvels how the grill is the one he built of cinder blocks,
how the fire roars up to sear the sliced flank steak
marinated in vodka and cherry juice, how it grills the
shish kebobs, vegetables like bright, skewered jewels,
yet there's no blast of heat to his face.

Everyone is invited: Mom's parents—Mary's depression, Julius's
deafness, gone. Her favorite uncle, Bernard, still looking
like Jerry Garcia, only handsomer, the cousin-aunts
from Montreal, Rosie and Irene, and Dad's parents Helen and Frank,
who astonish him by giving big bear hugs.
Mom brings out a tray of dishes and calls, "Let's eat!"

My Don ushers his folks to the redwood picnic table,
shiny as the day purchased, no splinters, no need to varnish.
Leans down to receive my mother's smooch. The mothers air-kiss,
the fathers shake hands. Ice tea is poured, cubes tinkle,
beer cans cracked open. Then Bernard says
in his richest synagogue voice, "Let's remember the ones
we left behind." And for a moment each of us
they loved on earth feels inexplicably blessed.

Carcass
> *for Grandma Mary, Thanksgiving over*

The bones rise up to sing
of hunger and the making of soup:

Let each sinew loosen in time's cauldron,
let the parched skin drink.
Let the vinegar bowls of hips shift
and dance, bones roiling in the pot;
salt draws out their marrow.
Let the roots—sweet when boiled—bob,
memories like feathered flecks of green
fly to the top, where the foamy waves of scum become
an ocean: the rising sun lays down its buttergold.

Only when your bones soften, may they be turned
to earth. So say our mothers' mothers:
Even in death, what feeds us is not lost.

My Coney Island

In dreams I see bathhouses like craggy ruined castles,
sky and sea where windows used to be.
A street of broken bungalows
leads to the beach, brown fishmeal sand, water
the impossible turquoise of the Aegean
where the Greeks began, and also my story,
under the boardwalk at night,
my mother and father pressed closer and closer
in the chilling sand after day's heat.

The rides, midway, barkers are silent,
people eating quietly at stands—Nathan's
hotdogs, raw clams, kasha knishes at Schatzkin's—
milling about or peopling the beach, animated
with no noise. In dreams, the only sound I hear
is the surf's roar, creation's bray, white-fingered,
looming waves grabbing me back to the avenues,
Surf, Neptune, Mermaid, land where my parents
played and I began, begin again.

Notes

The title "Not Just Any Old Food," was taken from a line in a Sharon Olds poem "The Missing Boy."

The form of "Song of Coney Island," was modeled after García Lorca's "Song of the Black Cubans."

The title of "Romance Alfómbrico (a word I coined in Spanish, meaning "of the carpet")," was modeled after, and the italicized lines were taken from, García Lorca's "Romance Somnámbulo."

Additional Acknowledgments

This book has been many years in the making. Some of the people who helped shape my writing are now gone: John Montague, the singing Irish poet, whose poetry workshops at the NYS Writers' Institute encouraged me when I started writing poetry again; Steve Orlen, first supervisor in the Warren Wilson MFA program, who pushed me to experiment; and Paul Elisha, paterfamilias of my long-running poetry workshop family.

Deep gratitude and thanks to the wonderful poets and teachers of the Warren Wilson MFA program, including my other teachers: Joan Aleshire, Debra Allbery, Marianne Boruch, and Eleanor Wilner.

To the members of my longstanding poetry workshop, thank you for being my first audience and editors. We laughed, we cried, we went to each other's celebrations and sad times. I still hear your voices when I edit my work: Sara Wiest, Joe Krausman, Ba Kaiser, Stu Bartow, Miriam Herrera, Anne Settel, and Barbara Ungar.

Appreciation and many thanks go to Joan Aleshire, who reviewed a larger manuscript from which this chapbook was taken and who patiently engaged with me in dialogue.

To the people in my life who listened to me and to my poems, no words can adequately express my gratitude, but without you, my life would have been immeasurably poorer: Bob Cutler, Jack O'Connor, Chris Balk, Laura Nash, Marta Jaremko, Richard Gotti, Deborah Foss, Beth Berry, Don Howard, and my Unity family. And for technical support in manuscript-processing as well as in life, a partner in silliness as well as intellectual pursuits, special thanks to Mark French. I am astonished and grateful we found each other.

Susan E. Oringel is a poet and writer, a teacher of creative writing, and a psychologist in private practice in the NYS Capital District. A graduate of the Warren Wilson M.F.A. program, she has published in various literary journals such as *Blueline, The Maryland Poetry Review* (second prize in the Egan Memorial Poetry Contest), *snowapple, crania, the writers community news,* and the National Council of Teachers of English *English Journal.* She has also served as co-translator of a collection of Latin American poetry: *Messengers of Rain*, published by Groundwoods Press, 2002 and 2011. Her chapbook manuscripts *How The Body* and *My Coney Island* were finalists in the Slapering Hol' Press 1997 and 2017 competitions. Fellowships and awards include Individual Artist award from the Albany-Schenectady League of Arts, a fellowship from the Vermont Studio Center, and an SOS award sponsored by the New York State Council of the Arts. She most recently taught creative writing at Hudson Valley Community College for fourteen years and previously taught writing at Empire State College and Schenectady Community College.

www.ingramcontent.com/pod-product-compliance
Lightning Source LLC
LaVergne TN
LVHW041507070426
835507LV00012B/1391